Barack Obama

President of the United States

Blane Conklin, Ph.D.

Consultant

Marcus McArthur, Ph.D.
Department of History
Saint Louis University

Publishing Credits

Dona Herweck Rice, *Editor-in-Chief*
Lee Aucoin, *Creative Director*
Chris McIntyre, M.A.Ed., *Editorial Director*
Torrey Maloof, *Associate Editor*
Neri Garcia, *Senior Designer*
Stephanie Reid, *Photo Researcher*
Rachelle Cracchiolo, M.S.Ed., *Publisher*

Image Credits

cover Shutterstock, Inc.; p.1 Shutterstock, Inc.; p.4 Newscom; p.5 The Library of Congress; p.6 (top) Shutterstock, Inc.; p.6 (bottom) Corbis; p.7 Corbis; p.8 Newscom; p.9 The Library of Congress; p.10 (top) The Library of Congress; p.10 (bottom) Shutterstock, Inc.; p.11 Newscom; p.12 Corbis; p.13 (left) Public Domain; p.13 (right) The Library of Congress; p.14 (top) Newscom; p.14 (bottom) Corbis; p.15 Getty Images; p.16 Newscom; p.17 (left) United States Defense Department; p.17 (right) Flickr; p.18 Newscom; p.19 Newscom; p.20 Shutterstock, Inc.; p.21 (left) Newscom; p.21 (right) Newscom; p.22 (top, left) The Library of Congress; p.22 (top, right) Shutterstock, Inc.; p.22 (bottom) Shutterstock, Inc.; p.23 Shutterstock, Inc.; p.24 (left) Shutterstock, Inc.; p.24 (right) Shutterstock, Inc.; p.25 Getty Images; p.26 Shutterstock, Inc.; p.27 Newscom; p.28 Newscom; p.29 (top, left) Newscom; p.29 (top, right) Newscom;]p.29 (bottom, left) Shutterstock, Inc.; p.29 (bottom, right) Shutterstock, Inc.; p.32 (left) Shutterstock, Inc.; p.32 (right) Getty Images

Teacher Created Materials
5301 Oceanus Drive
Huntington Beach, CA 92649-1030
http://www.tcmpub.com

ISBN 978-1-4333-1522-0

Table of Contents

Change in America

On November 4, 2008, Americans elected a new president. He was a United States **senator** from the state of Illinois (il-uh-NOI). His name was Barack Obama.

Just a few years before, most Americans had never heard of Barack Obama. He was young. He had done most of his work in Chicago. He knew that running for president would be difficult. But, he had a way of connecting with people. His message was simple: change was needed in America, and change would come if people worked together.

Obama was **inaugurated** (in-AW-gyuh-rey-ted) as the nation's 44th president on January 20, 2009. He took the **oath of office**. He gave a speech on the steps of the Capitol in Washington, DC. Then, he and his wife, Michelle, led a parade down Pennsylvania Avenue to the White House.

President Obama giving a speech

Dr. Martin Luther King Jr.

Obama was the first African American to be president of the United States. In itself, that was a change. He was from a different **political party** than the previous president, George W. Bush. That was another change. But the man himself, like the 43 presidents before him, has his own special story.

He Had a Dream

Dr. Martin Luther King Jr. once dreamed of a time when his children would "not be judged by the color of their skin, but by the content of their character." Barack Obama, too, did not want people to vote for or against him because of his color or race. He wanted people to vote for him because of his ideas and his character.

The Youngest President?

Obama is the fifth youngest person to become president. He was 47 years old. The youngest person to become president was Theodore Roosevelt. He was 42 years old when he was inaugurated. The United States Constitution says that a person must be at least 35 years old to become president.

Hawaiian Birthday

Barack Obama was born in Hawaii just two years after it became a state. It was the 50th state and entered the union on August 21, 1959.

A Big Family

Obama's family in Africa is part of the Luo (loo-OH) people. This is an **ethnic** group of more than three million people in Kenya. President Obama has six half-**siblings** from his father's side and one half-sibling from his mother's side.

Obama was born in Honolulu, Hawaii.

A young Obama posing with his father

Growing Up

A Different Perspective

Obama's father was a black man from Kenya, a country in Africa. His name was Barack Hussein (hoo-SEYN) Obama. He gave this same name to his son. Many members of his family were **Muslims** (MUHZ-limz). They practiced the religion of Islam (is-LAHM). The name *Hussein* is very common among Muslims.

Obama's mother was a white woman from the state of Kansas. Her name was Ann Dunham. Her father served in World War II. Her mother worked in a factory during the war.

The president's parents met at the University of Hawaii in 1960. Obama was born in Honolulu, Hawaii, on August 4, 1961. He did not see much of his father when he was younger. His father had left Hawaii to attend Harvard University. Later, Obama's father returned to Kenya. His father died in a car accident when Obama was 21 years old. His mother lived until 1995, when she died of cancer.

Being born in a family with both a black and a white parent was an unusual thing in the 1960s. It gave Obama a different **perspective** from someone with parents of the same race. He said that it allowed him to better understand the differences between African Americans and white people in America.

Obama with his mother, Ann Dunham

A Different Childhood

Obama's parents separated when he was only two years old. His mother married a university student from Indonesia (in-duh-NEE-zhuh). When Obama was six years old, the family moved to this foreign country. He attended school in Jakarta (juh-KAHR-tuh), the capital of Indonesia.

Obama quickly learned that the world was very different outside Hawaii. Chickens ran through the streets. Dogs and snakes were eaten. Monkeys screamed at you from the trees above. It was a whole new world of new languages, new religions, and new customs.

When he was ten, Obama moved back to Hawaii. He and his mother lived with his grandparents from then on. But, living in a foreign country showed Obama that the world was bigger than he had imagined.

Obama sits with his half-sister, Maya Soetoro, and his mother and stepfather.

The March on Washington for Civil Rights

Many African American leaders have been from southern states. This is where the **civil rights** struggle was greatest. It was where many battles of the United States Civil War were fought. Hawaii is very far from all this. Obama felt what it was like to be a **minority**. But he had a different experience from many African Americans living in the South.

A New Generation

Obama was the first president to be born after 1946. He was not even born when African Americans were struggling for civil rights during the 1940s and 1950s. He was only six years old when Dr. Martin Luther King Jr. was killed.

Rosa Parks

In 1955 in Montgomery, Alabama, an African American woman refused to give up her seat on a bus to a white person. Her name was Rosa Parks. She was arrested for her actions. This was one of the most important events in the history of civil rights in America. People became outraged and joined together to fight for civil rights. This happened just six years before Obama was born.

Andrew Young

Andrew Young

While Obama was in high school in Hawaii, African American **politicians** made important progress. In 1972, Andrew Young was elected to Congress from the state of Georgia. He was the first African American to be elected to Congress from Georgia since 1898. Mr. Young had been a friend of Dr. Martin Luther King Jr.

Classes for a Politician

At Columbia University, Obama studied political science. Political science is the study of government and politics. Obama learned a lot about how people from different nations with different governments relate to one another.

Getting an Education

Obama did not grow up in a wealthy family. However, he attended a very good school in Honolulu. This is where he began to learn the history of African Americans in the United States. He never thought it was strange that his father was black and his mother was white.

Obama felt at home with both white and black people. Yet many people around him were comfortable only with people of the same skin color as themselves. This was confusing to Obama.

Columbia University, New York City

Obama in Punahou High School in Honolulu, Hawaii

Obama thought about these things a lot. Sometimes it was too difficult to think about race. Growing up is hard for everyone. The same was true for Obama.

When he graduated from high school, Obama went to college in Los Angeles, California. For his first two years, he went to Occidental (ok-si-DEN-tuhl) College. Then he went to Columbia University in New York City. He graduated from Columbia in 1983.

Life in Chicago

Choosing a Profession

People would ask Obama what he was going to do after college. He told them he wanted to be a **community organizer**. Not many people knew what that meant. To Obama, it meant helping people improve their lives. It meant helping them learn to help themselves.

After Obama graduated from college, he stayed in New York City for two more years. In 1985, he went to Chicago, Illinois. His dream of being a community organizer was coming true. He worked to improve the lives of people on the south side of Chicago. He helped people who had lost their jobs. He helped them learn new skills and find new jobs. He also helped high school students prepare for college. Obama helped people have more control over where they lived.

Obama as president of the *Harvard Law Review*

Jesse Jackson was also a community organizer.

Harvard Law School

After three years in Chicago, Obama decided to go back to school. He thought this would make him a better community organizer. So, he went to Harvard Law School in 1988. Obama did something that no African American had ever done. He became the president of the *Harvard Law Review*. The *Harvard Law Review* is a journal published by the students at Harvard. It includes legal articles about the Supreme Court. This was an important honor, and it put Obama in the national news.

A Role Model

One of the people who worked toward civil rights with Dr. Martin Luther King Jr. was Jesse Jackson. He was a community organizer. Jackson helped improve the lives of people living in big cities. In 1984, he ran for president of the United States. When Obama was a university student, he listened to Jackson speak in New York City.

A Book of Dreams

After going to law school, Obama wrote his first book. It is called *Dreams from My Father*. In it, he tells the story of his life. It tells about his struggle to make sense of his life as a **multiracial** American.

Oprah Winfrey

Oprah Winfrey

Chicago is the home of Oprah Winfrey. She became popular during the time Obama lived in the city. She is a successful businesswoman. In fact, she was the richest African American of the 20th century! She later helped Obama with his run for the presidency.

Mrs. Obama

Mrs. Obama graduated from Harvard Law School in 1988. Just like her husband, she knew she wanted to help others in her community. One of Mrs. Obama's jobs was associate dean of student services for the University of Chicago. As associate dean, she helped start the university's first **community service** program.

Starting a Family

While Obama was at law school, he spent his summers in Chicago. He worked for a law office there. That first summer in 1989, he met Michelle Robinson. She was working at the same law office. In 1992, Robinson and Obama were married.

When Obama finished law school in 1991, he moved back to Chicago. Obama continued to work as a community organizer. But now, he did it as a lawyer. He worked to ensure the civil rights of people in Chicago. He also worked to help improve neighborhoods in the city.

Mr. and Mrs. Obama on their wedding day

Obama with his wife, Michelle, and their daughters, Sasha and Malia

At this time, Obama was also a university professor. He taught law school at the University of Chicago. He did this from 1992 until 2004. He taught classes about the United States Constitution.

The Obamas had two daughters who were born in Chicago. In 1998, their first daughter, Malia (muh-LEE-uh), was born. Their second daughter, Sasha, was born in 2001. The Obama family lived in the Hyde Park neighborhood of Chicago. This is on the south side of the city. The University of Chicago is located in this area.

Vote for Obama

Running for State Senate

In 1996, Obama ran for office for the first time. He wanted people to vote for him in an **election**. He won and was elected to the state senate of Illinois. As a state senator, Obama helped make laws for the state of Illinois. One of the laws was meant to fight **corruption**. Some politicians made laws that only helped people who gave them money. This law tried to stop that. Obama also worked on laws that helped poor and working families.

Obama was reelected to the Illinois senate twice. He helped pass laws for health care and worker's rights. Obama was a state senator until 2004.

Obama was a state senator in Illinois.

Condoleezza Rice

Secretary of State Colin Powell

In 2000, Obama ran for a seat in the **House of Representatives**. He lost that election to another African American **candidate**, Bobby L. Rush. Most people voting in that election were African American. Many of those people did not think that Obama knew enough about their lives. Even though Obama is an African American, many African Americans have a much different history. Many are descended from African slaves who were brought to America hundreds of years ago. Obama knew he needed to convince African Americans that he understood them and their issues.

Two Firsts

During the presidency of George W. Bush, two African Americans served as the Secretary of State. Colin Powell was the first African American to serve as secretary of state. Condoleezza Rice was the second. She was also the second woman to have that job.

Mr. Mayor

The first African American to be the mayor of Chicago was Harold Washington. He was the mayor from 1983 until he died in 1987. Obama was working as a community organizer in Chicago during that time.

Famous Line

This is a famous line from Obama's 2004 speech: "There is not a Black America and a White America and Latino America and Asian America—there's the *United* States of America."

State Senator vs. United States Senator

A state senator represents his or her state on a local level. A United States senator represents his or her state on a federal level. This means the senator travels to Washington, DC, and works with the senators from the other states. There are only two United States senators per state.

Obama gives a speech at the Democratic Convention in 2004.

America, Meet Obama

In 2004, Obama ran for a new office. He wanted to become a United States senator. There are 100 senators, two from each of the 50 states. He wanted to be one of the two senators from Illinois. Another election was also taking place in 2004, the election for president of the United States. That summer, the two political parties met to **nominate** (NOM-uh-nayt) their candidate. The Republican Party nominated George W. Bush. The Democratic Party nominated John Kerry.

At the Democratic meeting, Obama was given an opportunity to speak. At that time, hardly anyone outside of Chicago had heard of Obama. It was a great way for people to learn more about him. Obama gave a powerful speech. It was well received. After that speech, he became a **sensation**. People wanted to know more about Obama. Many began to wonder if Obama might someday run for president.

In the speech, Obama told the story of his life. He talked about how America promised opportunity and freedom. He said that his story was only possible in America. He said that Americans should not let their differences keep them from making America a better place for everyone.

John Kerry and George W. Bush both ran for president in 2004.

Senator Obama

Obama won his election in 2004. He was now a United States Senator from Illinois. He was the only African American in the Senate. He was the third African American to be elected to the Senate in more than 120 years!

This new job took Obama to Washington, DC. But since senators represent the people of their state, he also spent lots of time in Illinois. His family stayed in Chicago. Obama rented an apartment in Washington. He would stay there whenever he had to be in the capital.

The term of a United States senator is six years. Obama served less than four years, because in 2008, he was elected president of the United States. During his four years in the Senate, Obama helped write a law to reduce certain kinds of military weapons. He passed a law that helped people see how the government is spending their money. In many of his efforts, Senator Obama worked with senators of the other political party. His belief is that real change only comes when people listen to one another and work together.

The State Capitol Building in Washington, DC, is where senators meet.

United States Senator Carol Moseley-Braun

Famous First

The second African American to be elected to the Senate since the 1870s was also from Illinois. In 1992, Carol Moseley-Braun was elected to the United States Senate. She was the first African American woman to become a senator. She was also the first woman senator from Illinois.

A Book of Hope

Obama wrote his second book in 2006. It reflected the ideas he presented in his 2004 speech. The title of the book is *The Audacity of Hope*.

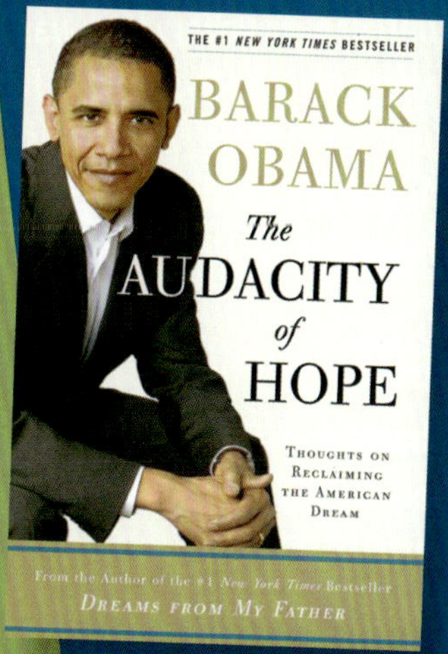

President Abraham Lincoln

Obama gives a speech during the primary elections.

Lincoln's Speech

The famous speech that Abraham Lincoln gave in 1858 is called the "House Divided" speech. In it, he talks about the conflict over slavery that was taking place in the nation. He quoted the Bible, which says, "A house divided against itself cannot stand."

Another First

Obama won the presidential nomination for the Democratic Party. It was the first time an African American had been nominated by one of the big political parties.

Senator Hillary Clinton

Long Race to the White House

Primary Elections

After being a United States Senator for only two years, Obama announced that he was running to be president of the United States. It was February of 2007. It was almost two years before the presidential election. Obama made his announcement in Springfield, Illinois. It was in the same spot where Abraham Lincoln gave a famous speech in 1858.

The **campaign** (kam-PEYN) for president begins with the **primary elections**. During this time, each political party has smaller elections in many different states. In this way, each side chooses who will run in the **general election**. For the Democratic Party, there were many people running against each other in the primary elections. One of these people was Hillary Clinton, the wife of former President Bill Clinton. She was a senator from the state of New York.

After more than a year of primary elections, the decision was made. Senator Obama had won more votes than Senator Clinton. Obama would be the Democratic candidate in the general election in November 2008. The Republican candidate would be Senator John McCain from the state of Arizona.

Senator John McCain

Obama or McCain?

In the summer of 2008, the two political parties had chosen their leaders. For the Democrats, it was Senator Barack Obama from Illinois. For the Republicans, it was Senator John McCain from Arizona.

The two candidates tried hard to get people to vote for them. They put commercials on television. They made speeches across the nation. They chose running mates. These were the people who would be vice president. Obama chose Senator Joseph Biden from Delaware. McCain chose Governor Sarah Palin from Alaska.

Senator Joseph Biden

Governor Sarah Palin

Obama gives his victory speech.

Obama and McCain had three **debates**. In these debates, they argued about who would be better to lead the nation. They debated the war in Iraq. They debated who had better ideas for the environment and for health care. They debated who would be better for the **economy**.

On November 4, 2008, the people finally made their choice. Almost 70 million people voted for Obama. Almost 60 million people voted for John McCain. The winner was Obama. He was the first African American to be elected president of the United States.

Victory Speech

This is a line from Obama's speech on election night, November 4, 2008: "For that is the true genius of America—that America can change. Our union can be perfected. And what we have already achieved gives us hope for what we can and must achieve tomorrow."

None of the Above?

Nearly two million people voted for other candidates for president. These candidates included Ralph Nader, Bob Barr, and Cynthia McKinney. Ms. McKinney represented the Green Party. She was the first African American woman elected to the House of Representatives from the state of Georgia.

President Barack Obama

The election of a president takes place in November. But the person elected does not actually become the president until Inauguration (in-aw-gyuh-REY-shuhn) Day. This takes place on January 20 of the year following the election.

On January 20, 2009, more than one million people attended the celebration in Washington, DC. Millions more watched the inauguration on television and the Internet. Former presidents attended the ceremony, including President George W. Bush. This was his last day as president. Members of the Supreme Court and members of Congress attended. There were famous musicians, poets, and many other celebrities as well.

Obama being sworn in as president of the United States

More than one million people were at the inauguration in Washington, DC.

Many big challenges faced the new president. The economy of the United States was in a **crisis**. The nation was in the middle of two wars—one in Iraq and one in Afghanistan. **Terrorism** was a constant threat. The United States was also trying to solve energy problems. The world was trying to deal with **global warming**.

President Obama said that everyone in the United States should work together to meet these challenges. The president faced a long and hard road. But for Barack Obama, his family, and the entire nation, this one day was a day to celebrate.

New Challenges

This is a line from President Obama's Inaugural Speech: "Our challenges may be new . . . but those values upon which our success depends—honesty and hard work, courage and fair play, tolerance and curiosity, loyalty and patriotism—these things are old. These things are true."

Defining Moment

An important moment for President Obama and the United States came on May 1, 2011. After nearly 10 years of searching, the terrorist behind the attacks on September 11, 2001, Osama bin Laden, was found and killed.

President Barack Obama and members of the national security team receive updates on the mission to find Osama bin Laden.

Home Sweet Home

Life at home is very different for a president and his family. They get to live in the White House. The White House is not your typical house. It has its own gym and tennis court. It even has an indoor bowling alley and movie theater! There are 132 rooms and 35 bathrooms! But, the Obamas have tried to make the White House feel like a home for their two daughters.

While living at the White House, Malia and Sasha live like other kids. They have had to do their chores. They have had to clean their rooms, just as they did when they lived in Chicago. They have gone to school and done their homework. But, they have had fun, too. Friends have visited for sleepovers and parties!

As the president's wife, Michelle Obama is the First Lady of the United States. At the White House, she has worked hard to teach her daughters about the importance of good health and nutrition. They helped her plant a garden at the White House. This provides **organic** food for family meals. It is also used to help feed needy families in Washington, DC.

Mrs. Obama working in the garden with student volunteers

President Obama and First Lady Michelle with their daughters, Sasha and Malia

President Obama

Actor Will Smith

Bo

The "First Puppy"

President Obama promised his daughters he would get them a dog when the race for the presidency was over. Their dream came true when they got Bo, a fluffy black dog with white paws. Bo is a Portuguese (pohr-chuh-GEEZ) Water Dog.

Lights, Camera, Action!

If a movie were ever made about President Obama's life, which actor would best portray the president? The president himself would like actor Will Smith to play the role. He says he has the right ears for the part.

Glossary

campaign—all the effort that a person makes to run in an election

candidate—a person who runs in an election; someone to vote for in an election

civil rights—the rights that every citizen should receive; all of the rights promised by the Constitution of the United States

community organizer—someone who works to improve the lives of people in a community

community service—work done for free for the common good of society

corruption—actions that are against the law; dishonest behavior

crisis—an emergency

debates—discussions or arguments between two or more people over certain issues

economy—anything having to do with money, work, buying, and selling

election—an event where people vote for candidates to an office

ethnic—a group of people who have similar characteristics

general election—the final election between candidates of different parties

global warming—the changes in Earth's climate because of pollution

House of Representatives—the lower legislative branch of the United States government

inaugurated—sworn into office to begin a president's term

minority—a smaller group of people within a larger group

multiracial—someone who has parents of different races

Muslims—people who follow the religion of Islam

nominate—to choose a candidate to represent your party

oath of office—a promise to obey the laws and to behave as an elected leader should

organic—food that has not been treated with man-made chemicals

perspective—a point of view; a way of looking at things

political party—a group of people who share certain beliefs and ideas about how to lead

politicians—people who are elected, or want to be elected, to an office

primary elections—smaller elections between candidates in the same party

senator—an elected member of the senate, who makes laws

sensation—a cause of excitement

siblings—brothers or sisters

terrorism—the use of violence and threats to achieve a goal

Index

Your Turn!

On January 20, 2009, more than one million people gathered in Washington, DC, to celebrate Barack Obama's inauguration. On that day Obama became America's first African American president.

Fast Forward

Imagine that one day in the future your child sees a video clip of Barack Obama's inauguration. He or she might ask, "What was the big deal about that day?" Write the answer you would give to your child. Use facts from the reading to make your explanation clear.